D0426739

The Baby in the Basket

© 1994 by
THE MOODY BIBLE INSTITUTE
OF CHICAGO

This story has been extracted from
Read-Aloud Bible Stories, vol. 4

Illustrated by
H. Kent Puckett

Printed in Mexico

MOODY PRESS

One day the bad king said,
"I don't want
any more boy babies.
Take all the boy babies
and throw them away."

Now this mommy
and this daddy
had a pretty baby boy.
They loved him.
Did they want
to throw him away?
Oh, no.

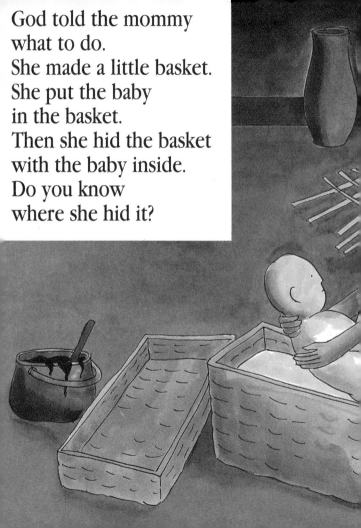

God told the mommy
what to do.
She made a little basket.
She put the baby
in the basket.
Then she hid the basket
with the baby inside.
Do you know
where she hid it?

She hid it
in the tall grass
beside the water.
Who would ever look
for a baby THERE?
Nobody.

The mommy said to Big Sister, "You stand here. You make sure NOBODY takes this basket."

Now the king—
remember him?—
the king had a big girl.
She was the princess.

One day the princess
went for a walk,
step, step, step.
Her helpers went with her,
step, step, step.
They all went walking
beside the water.

They walked up,
step, step, step.
They walked down,
step, step, step.
Then the princess
saw the basket.

"What's THAT
in the grass?"
(*We* know what it was,
don't we?)
The princess said,
"Bring it here to me."
Oh, my!

One of her helpers
brought the basket.
The princess
looked inside and—
what's this?
A BABY BOY!
The baby started to cry.
"Oh," the princess said. "Oh."
(Do you think
she liked him?)

God told Big Sister
what to do.
Big Sister came fast.
Big Sister said,
"Shall I find somebody
to take care of the baby
for you?"
The princess said—

"Yes."
And off ran Big Sister.
(Go fast, Big Sister!
Go fast!)
Off ran Big Sister
to find the baby's mommy.

The princess said,
'Take care of this baby,
and I will give you pennies."
The mommy was happy.
She didn't care
about the pennies.
She just wanted her baby.
She picked him up,
and she took him home.

When the baby got bigger,
the princess gave him a name.
She said, "His name will be—
MOSES."
And it was.

What did you learn?

God told the mommy what to do.
God told Big Sister what to do.
God knew how to take care of
baby Moses.

He knows how to take care of
you too.

About the Author

Ella K. Lindvall (A.B., Taylor University; Wheaton College; Northern Illinois University) is a mother and former elementary school teacher. She is the author of *The Bible Illustrated for Little Children*, and *Read-Aloud Bible Stories*, volumes I, II, III, and IV.